MI PRIMER ABECEDARIO

Arabic-Spanish

ب

Baa

BATARIQ   PINGÜINO

ب
ب
ب
بطريق
بطريق

Arabic-Spanish

ث

Thaa

THUEBAN　　　SERPIENTE

ث

ث

ث

ثعبان

ثعبان

Arabic-Spanish

ح
Haa

HISAN   CABALLO

ح
ح
ح
حصان
حصان

Arabic-Spanish

Daal

DAWADA   GUSANO

د

د

د

دودة

دودة

Arabic-Spanish

ذ

Dhaal

DHIL　　　　COLA

ذ

ذ

ذ

ذيل

ذيل

Arabic-Spanish

Seen

SANJAB   ARDILLA

س

س

س

سنجاب

سنجاب

Arabic-Spanish

ص

Saad

SARUKH   COHETE

ص

ص

ص

صاروخ

صاروخ

Arabic-Spanish

ش

Sheen

SHAMS DOM

ش

ش

ش

شمس

شمس

Arabic-Spanish

Tau

TABLA　　　　　TAMBOR

ط

ط

ط

طبلة

طبلة

Arabic-Spanish

ع
Ayn

EAYAN   OJO

ع

ع

ع

عين

عين

Arabic-Spanish

فـع   Faa

FIL   ELEFANTE

فع

فع

فع

فيل

فيل

Arabic-Spanish

Arabic-Spanish

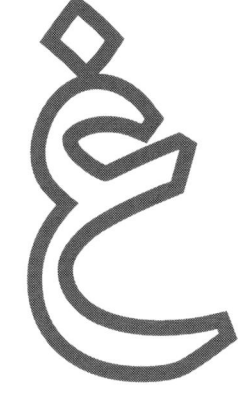

Ghain

GHURAB CUERVO

غ

غ

غ

غراب

غراب

Arabic-Spanish

Meem

MUZA   PLÁTANO

م

م

م

موزة

موزة

Arabic-Spanish

لق
Laam

ALLAQALAQ   CIGÜEÑA

لق

لق

لق

اللقلق

اللقلق

Arabic-Spanish

Noon ن

NAEAMA   AVESTRUZ

ن

ن

ن

نعامة

نعامة

Arabic-Spanish

ي
Yaa

YD　　　MANO

ي
ي
ي
يد
يد

Arabic-Spanish

و

Waow

WALAD   NIÑO

و

و

و

ولد

ولد

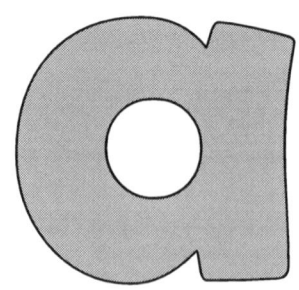

A for Apple

A for Ant

A for Alligator

B b

B for Bat B for Boy

B for Ball B for Bell

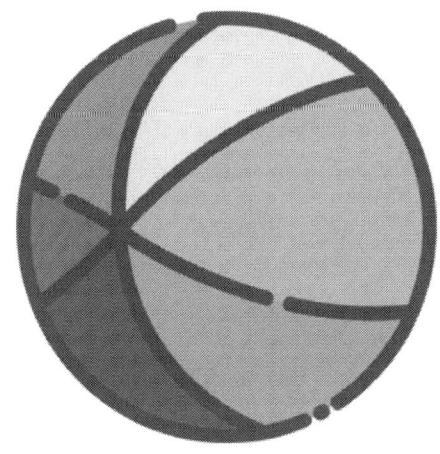
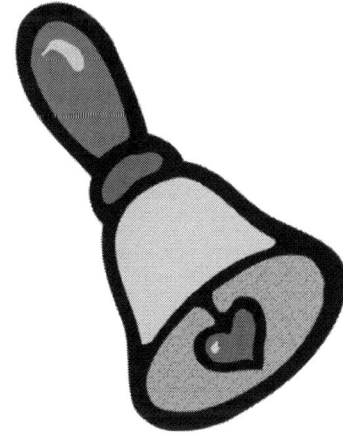

C c

C for Cat

C for Cow

C for Corn

C for Cake

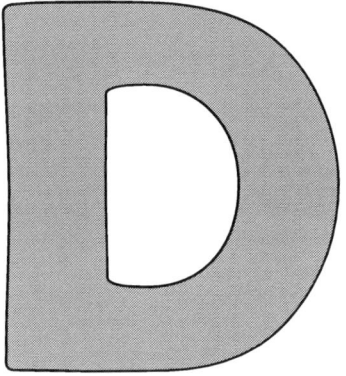 

D for Dog

D for Doll

D for Dish

D for Deer

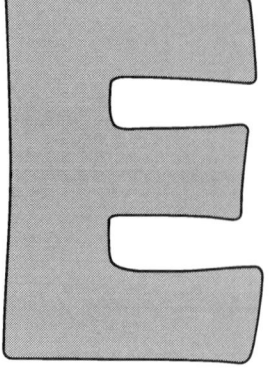 

E for Egg

E for Elephant

E for Eight

E for Eat

F for Fish   F for Frog

F for Flag   F for Fan

G g

G for Goat

G for Gum

G for Goose

G for Gun

H h

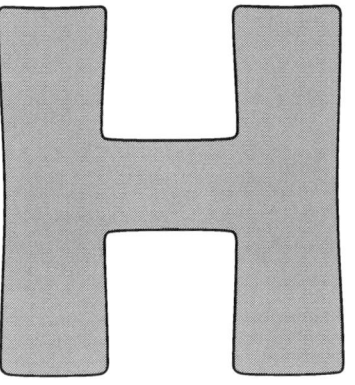
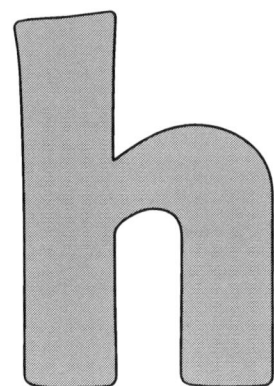

H for Horse

H for House

H for Hippo

H for Ham

I i

I for Ice-cream

I for Ice

I for Igloo

I for Iguana

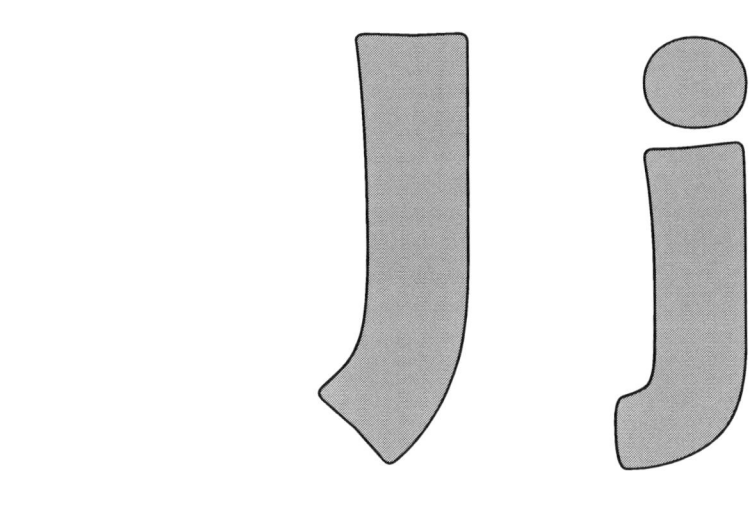

J for Jug

J for Jam

J for Jet

J for Jump

K k

K for King   K for Kangaroo

K for Kid   K for Knight

M m

M for Moon

M for Man

M for Monkey

M for Mouse

N n

N for Nut

N for Net

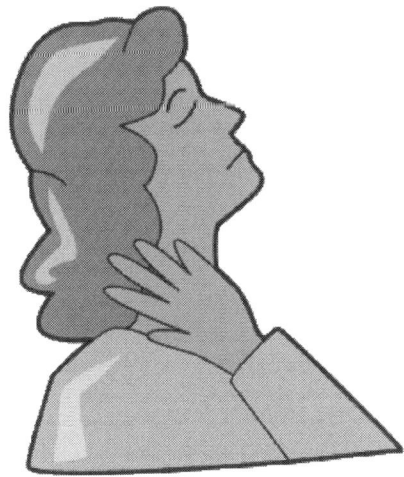
N for Neck

N for Nose

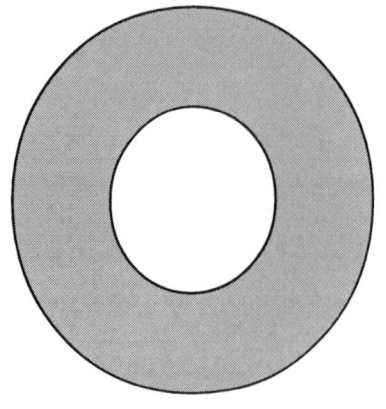
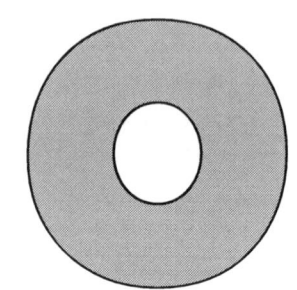

O for Octopus

O for Owl

O for Ox

O for Orange

P p

P for Penguin   P for Pig

P for Pot   P for Pan

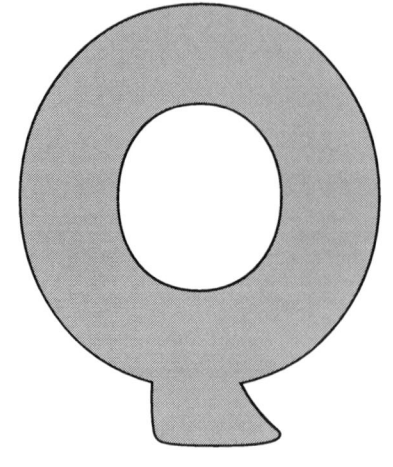

Q for Queen

Q for Quilt

Q for Quail

Q for Question

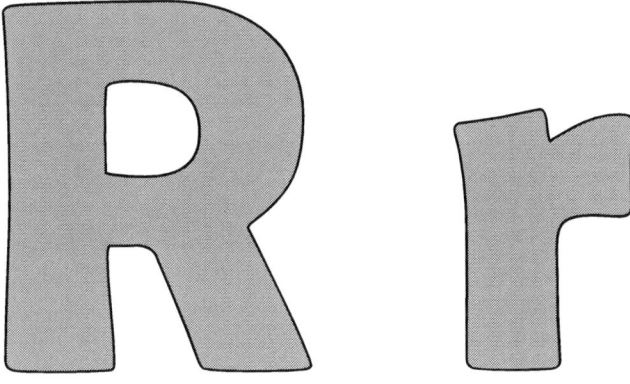

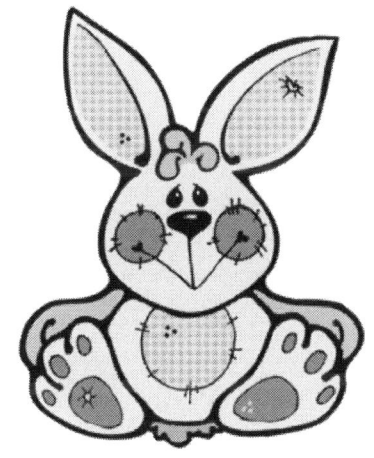
R for Rabbit

R for Rat

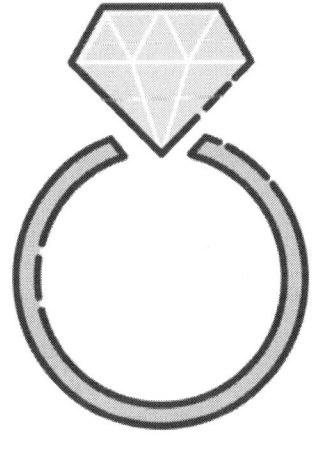
R for Ring

R for Ram

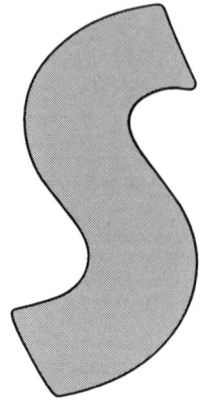 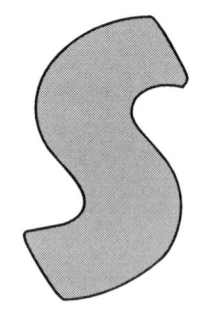

S for Sun   S for Sheep

S for Star   S for Snake

T t

T for Turtle

T for Tub

T for Toy

T for Tiger

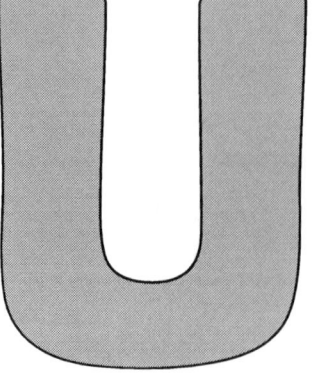 

U for Umbrella

U for Unicorn

U for Up

U for UFO

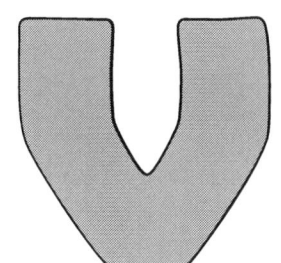

V for Van

V for Violin

V for Vase

U for Volcano

W for Whale

W for Walrus

W for Walk

W for Water

X for X'mas

X for Xylophone

X for Xray

Y y

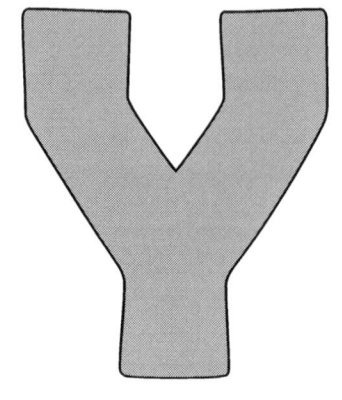

Y for Yak

Y for Yo-yo

Y for Yarn

Y for Yogurt

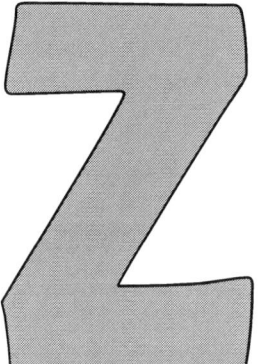 

Z for Zebra

Z for Zero

Z for Zoo

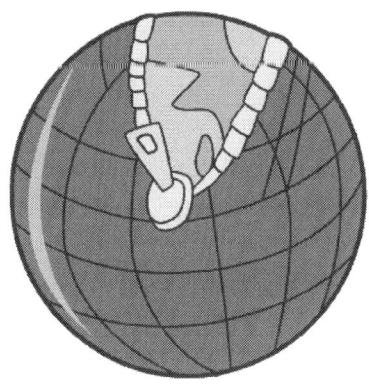

Z for Zipper

Name: _____

Date: _____

Name: _____

Date: _____

☆ ☆ ☆

B B B B B

b b b b b

B B B B B

B B B B B

B B B B B

Name: _____

Date: _____

☆ ☆ ☆

C C C C C

c c c c c

Name: _____

Date: _____

☆ ☆ ☆

Name: _____

Date: _____

Name: _____

Date: _____

☆ ☆ ☆

F f

Name: _____

Date: _____

☆ ☆ ☆

G g

Name: _____

Date: _____

☆ ☆ ☆

Name: _____

Date: _____

☆ ☆ ☆

I i

Name: _____

Date: _____

J J J J J J

j j j j j j

Name: _____
Date: _____

☆ ☆ ☆

K K K K K
k k k k k

Name: _____

Date: _____

Name: _____

Date: _____

☆ ☆ ☆

Name: _____

Date: _____

☆ ☆ ☆

N N N N N N

n n n n n n

Name: _____
Date: _____

O o

Name: _____

Date: _____

☆ ☆ ☆

P P P P P

p p p p p

Name: _____

Date: _____

☆ ☆ ☆

Name: _____

Date: _____

☆ ☆ ☆

R R R R R

r r r r r

Name: _____

Date: _____

☆ ☆ ☆

S S S S S

s s s s s

Name: _____

Date: _____

☆ ☆ ☆

Name: _____

Date: _____

☆ ☆ ☆

U U U U U

u u u u u

Name: _____

Date: _____

☆ ☆ ☆

Name: _____ ☆ ☆ ☆

Date: _____

WWWWWWWW

wwwwwww

Name: _____

Date: _____

X X X X X X

x x x x x x

Name: _____

Date: _____

☆ ☆ ☆

Name: _____

Date: _____

☆ ☆ ☆

Z Z Z Z Z Z

z z z z z z

UPPER-CASE

A

lower-case

a

These pictures begin with the letter A, a. Color the pictures.

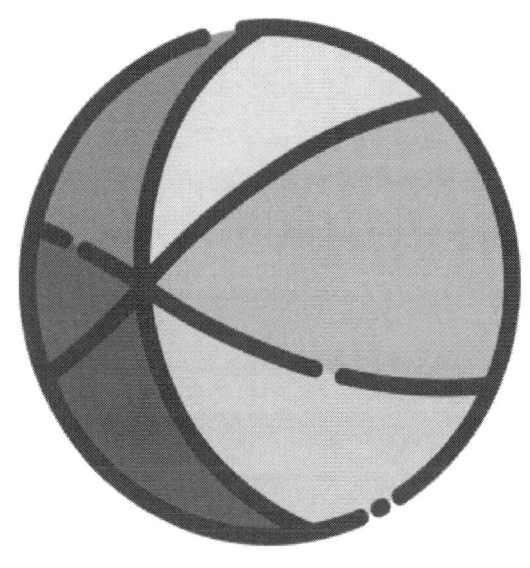

UPPER-CASE

B

lower-case

b

These pictures begin with the letter B,b. Color the pictures.

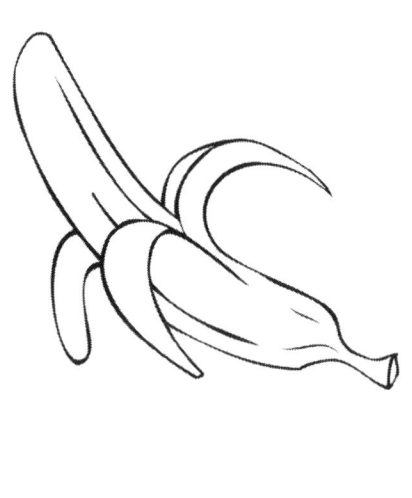

UPPER-CASE

C

lower-case

c

These pictures begin with the letter C,c. Color the pictures.

UPPER-CASE

lower-case

These pictures begin with the letter D,d. Color the pictures.

UPPER-CASE

E

lower-case

e

These pictures begin with the letter E,e. Color the pictures.

UPPER-CASE

 F

lower-case

f

These pictures begin with the letter F,f. Color the pictures.

UPPER-CASE

G

lower-case

g

These pictures begin with the letter G,g. Color the pictures.

UPPER-CASE

lower-case

These pictures begin with the letter H,h. Color the pictures.

UPPER-CASE

I

lower-case

i

These pictures begin with the letter I, i. Color the pictures.

UPPER-CASE

J

lower-case

j

These pictures begin with the letter J,j. Color the pictures.

UPPER-CASE

K

lower-case

k

These pictures begin with the letter K,k. Color the pictures.

UPPER-CASE

L

lower-case

l

These pictures begin with the letter L,l. Color the pictures.

UPPER-CASE

M

lower-case

m

These pictures begin with the letter M,m. Color the pictures.

UPPER-CASE

N

lower-case

n

These pictures begin with the letter N,n. Color the pictures.

UPPER-CASE

O

lower-case

o

These pictures begin with the letter O,o. Color the pictures.

UPPER-CASE

lower-case

These pictures begin with the letter P,p. Color the pictures.

UPPER-CASE

Q

lower-case

q

These pictures begin with the letter Q,q. Color the pictures.

UPPER-CASE

R

lower-case

r

These pictures begin with the letter R,r. Color the pictures.

UPPER-CASE

S

lower-case

s

These pictures begin with the letter S,s. Color the pictures.

UPPER-CASE

T

lower-case

t

These pictures begin with the letter T,t. Color the pictures.

UPPER-CASE

U

lower-case

u

These pictures begin with the letter U,u. Color the pictures.

UPPER-CASE

lower-case

These pictures begin with the letter V,v. Color the pictures.

UPPER-CASE

W

lower-case

These pictures begin with the letter W,w. Color the pictures.

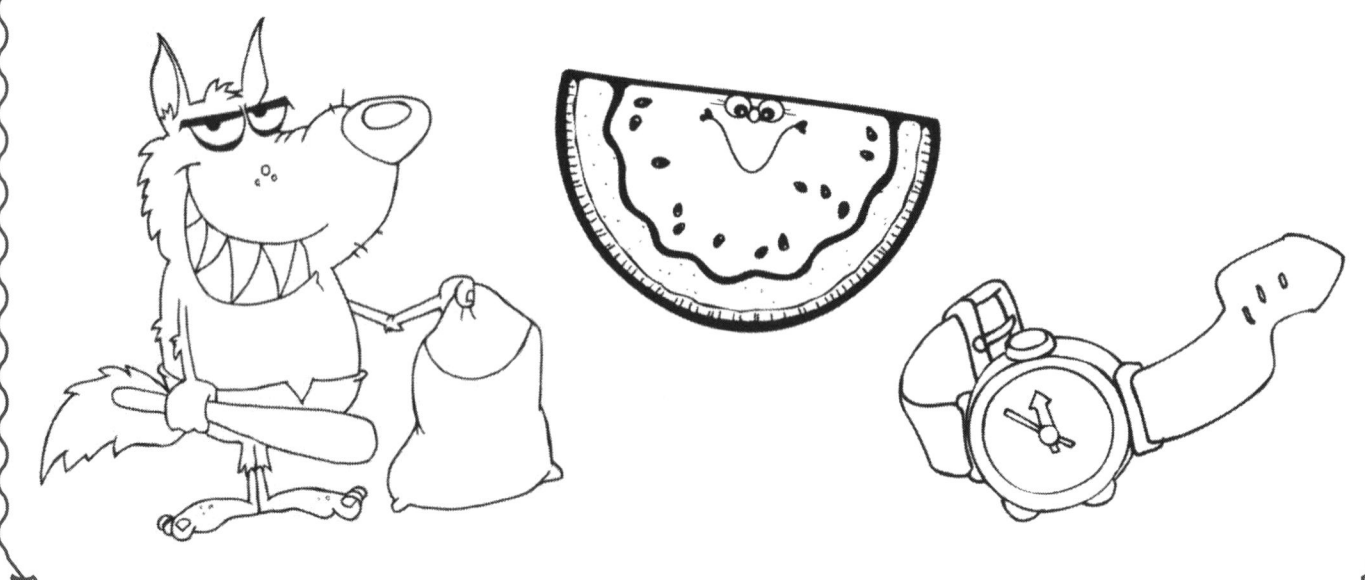

UPPER-CASE

X

lower-case

x

These pictures begin with the letter X,x. Color the pictures.

UPPER-CASE

Y

lower-case

y

These pictures begin with the letter Y,y. Color the pictures.

UPPER-CASE

Z

lower-case

z

These pictures begin with the letter Z,z. Color the pictures.

Made in the USA
Middletown, DE
10 May 2023